SCIENCE COOKERY

THROUGH

Liquids in Action

Peter Mellett
Jane Rossiter

FRANKLIN WATTS

New York • London • Toronto • Sydney

© Franklin Watts 1992

Franklin Watts, Inc.
95 Madison Avenue
New York, NY 10016

Library of Congress Cataloging-in-Publication Data

Mellett, P. (Peter), 1946-
    Liquids in action/by Peter Mellett and Jane Rossiter.
        p. cm. – (Science through cookery)
    Includes index.
    Summary: Examines the principles of liquids through the cooking of
a variety of recipes from different countries and cultures.
        ISBN 0–531–14235–3
        1. Cookery–Juvenile literature. 2. Liquids–Juvenile literature.
    [1. Cookery. 2. Liquids.] I. Rossiter. Jane. II. Title.
    III. Series.
    TX652.5.M37 1993
    532'.0078–dc20   92-7649
                                                            CIP AC

Senior editor: Hazel Poole
Series editor: Jane Walker
Designer: Ann Samuel
Illustrator: Annabel Milne
Photographer: Michael Stannard
Consultant: Margaret Whalley

The publisher would like to
thank the following children
for their participation in the
photography of this book:
Tom Brownrigg, Caroline
Rossiter, Alexander Rossiter,
Katie Samuel and Corinne
Smith-Williams.

Typeset by Spectrum, London
Printed in Singapore

Contents

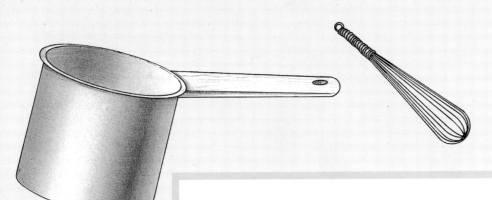

Introduction

Science Through Cookery is a new, simple, and fun approach to learning about science. In each book you will not only read about science, but you will also have first-hand experience of real science. By linking science topics with simple cookery recipes, you can learn about science and at the same time cook some delicious recipes. Science is fun when you finish up eating the results of your work!

About this book

In **Liquids in Action** you can read about water and other liquids. The book explains how liquids behave when heated or when a solid substance is added. Simple explanations of difficult terms, such as density and surface tension, help you to understand why some liquids will not mix.

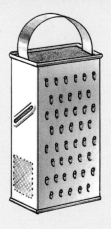

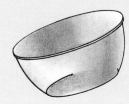

Liquids in Action explains important scientific principles with the help of clearly labeled diagrams and illustrations. The recipes offer a practical opportunity to gain a better understanding of the science you have just read about.

Each recipe has been carefully selected and written so that the cooking can be done with a minimum amount of adult supervision. Where the help of an adult is needed, for example when boiling a pot of water, this is clearly indicated.

The ingredients and equipment you will need are listed at the beginning of each recipe. They are easily obtainable and no special equipment is required. The step-by-step format of the recipes is easy to follow. Each step is illustrated with a photograph.

At the end of the book you will find a page of Further things to do. These are fun experiments and activities which are linked to many of the science concepts discussed in the book. A glossary of terms and an index are provided at the end of the book.

What is a liquid?

Eggs, bread, air, custard, and spoons, and everything else in the world are made up from matter. Matter can exist in three states: solid, liquid, or gas.

Wooden or metal spoons are solids. They are firm and keep their shape. When food is cooking, it gives off gases that we can smell. Gases spread out and completely fill the space they are in.

Milk, lemonade, and water are all liquids. They are runny and we can pour them from one container to

Banana milk shake

Ingredients
15 fl oz milk
1 banana
2 teaspoons sugar
a little grated nutmeg

Equipment

a measuring cup
a blender or food processor
a cutting board
a knife
a teaspoon
2 glasses

1 Measure the milk in the measuring cup. Peel the banana and chop it into pieces.

2 Put the milk, banana, and sugar into the blender or food processor. Switch it on and blend the ingredients together until the mixture is thick and frothy.

another. Liquids spread out to fill the lowest part of their containers. Liquids also have flat and level surfaces.

Matter takes up space and has mass. You can measure the mass of anything by weighing it. Some substances can exist in all three states. Depending on the temperature, water can exist as solid ice, as liquid water, or as a gas called steam.

Milk is a liquid, but 95 percent of milk is actually water. A tomato is a solid, but 95 percent of it is water. Your body is about 65 percent water. During your lifetime, you will take in about 60,000 quarts of water.

All your food contains water. Look how much water is in these foods:
- bread 30%
- steak 70%
- lettuce 95%
- potato 80%
- orange 85%

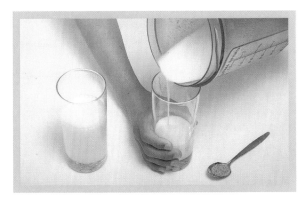

3 Pour the milk shake into two glasses, and sprinkle it with some grated nutmeg.

From a liquid to a gas

A kettle of boiling water gives off hot, steamy clouds. But if you look carefully, you will see a clear space right next to the spout. This clear space appears to be empty, but it actually contains a colorless gas called steam. When the water inside the kettle is heated, some of it turns into steam. The change from a liquid to a gas is called evaporation.

As the steam moves away from the spout, it cools and changes into tiny droplets of water. The change from a gas to a liquid is called condensation. The water droplets make up the steamy clouds you can see.

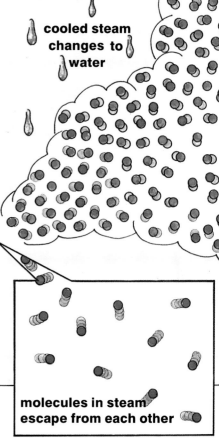

cooled steam changes to water

steam

molecules in steam escape from each other

Every substance is made up from tiny invisible pieces, or particles, called atoms. In most liquids, the atoms are joined together in separate groups called molecules.

Water is made from molecules. The molecules are all the same, and they are moving about freely all the time. The hotter the water, the faster the molecules are moving. Some of the molecules in boiling water are moving so fast that they escape completely from each other. The result is steam.

!

Evaporated milk is made by heating milk in a special container. Some of the water in the milk evaporates. It turns into a gas which is pumped away. The rest of the milk contains fats and solids which do not evaporate. They stay in the container and become evaporated milk.

In hot countries, seawater is used to make sea salt. The seawater flows into shallow pools. Heat from the sun evaporates the water, leaving behind solid salt.

Steamed vegetable bundles

Ingredients
4 large cabbage leaves
1 carrot
1 leek
1 celery stalk
salt and pepper

Equipment

a large pot, with a steamer
a cutting board
a knife
a bowl
a slotted spoon
4 toothpicks

1 Half fill the pot with water. Ask an adult to help you boil the water. Wash all the vegetables, and scrub the carrot and celery.

2 Carefully cut the hard stalk out of the end of the cabbage leaves.

3 Chop the carrot, leek, and celery into very small pieces. Put these into the bowl and season well with salt and pepper. Mix the ingredients together.

4 When the pot of water is boiling, ask an adult to help you lower the cabbage leaves into it. Boil for 1 minute. Carefully remove with the slotted spoon, and place on the cutting board.

5 Divide the vegetable mixture into four portions, and place some mixture on each leaf. Roll up the leaves to make bundles. Push a toothpick through each bundle.

6 Place the bundles carefully into the steamer and put it over the pot of simmering water. Cover the steamer with a lid.

7 Steam the bundles for 20 minutes. Remove them from the steamer and serve at once. The vegetables will be cooked but still quite firm.

From a liquid to a solid

Water is a runny liquid. But if you put some water in the freezer, it will turn into solid ice. What makes this happen?

The molecules in a liquid rush about and move freely past each other. When you cool a liquid, some heat energy is removed from it, making the molecules move more slowly.

When water is very cold, the molecules do not have enough energy to move about freely. They join together in groups and gently vibrate backward and forward. These groups make up crystals of ice. The crystals contain water molecules that are fixed in a regular pattern.

molecules in water move freely

molecules in ice join together

32°F — water

−23°F — fruit juice

248°F — toffee

Different liquids freeze at different temperatures. Water freezes at 32 degrees Fahrenheit (32°F for short). Fruit juice freezes at an even lower temperature (−23°F). Hot liquid toffee "freezes" (hardens) when the temperature falls below 248°F.

!

There were no electric refrigerators 200 years ago, but wealthy people still wanted cold drinks in the summer.

During the winter, their servants cut lumps of ice from a frozen river. They stored the ice in icehouses, which were large underground rooms covered with heavy blocks of stone and soil. Bales of straw were placed around the ice to keep out the warmth. The ice stayed solid for many months in the ice-houses.

Apricot yogurt ice

Ingredients
1 lb canned apricots
12 oz natural yogurt
2 egg whites
2 tablespoons soft brown sugar

Equipment

a can opener
a strainer
2 small bowls
a cutting board
a knife
a large bowl
an electric mixer
a tablespoon
a plastic container with a lid

1 Open the can of apricots. Place the strainer over a bowl and pour the apricots into the strainer.

2 Chop the drained apricots into small pieces. Spoon the yogurt into a bowl and add the chopped apricots. Mix untii the ingredients are thoroughly combined.

3 Separate the egg whites from the yolks. (You cannot beat the whites properly if any yolk is left behind.) Put the egg whites into the large bowl.

4 Beat the egg whites until they are stiff and no longer move about when you tilt the bowl.

5 Beat the sugar into the egg whites, one tablespoon at a time.

6 Pour the apricot and yogurt mixture into the bowl of beaten egg whites. Mix together gently but thoroughly until the ingredients are combined.

7 Spoon the mixture into the plastic container and freeze until it is solid (about 4 hours).

Liquids and heat energy

Jam is made by boiling a mixture of fruit and sugar. Some kinds of fruit contain too much water. If this water is not removed, the jam will be too runny.

When the mixture is boiled in a pot, the extra water turns into a gas called steam. Heat from the stove gives energy to the molecules in the jam mixture. This makes them move about more quickly. Water molecules are smaller and lighter than the other molecules in the mixture. As the mixture boils, the water evaporates and some molecules escape as steam.

If you boil milk very gently for a long time, all the water eventually escapes. The result is a white solid. This solid is the part of milk that does not boil away as steam. When this solid is mixed with some liquid water, the result is milk.

Dried food keeps for a very long time. In hot countries, fish, coconut, and fruits like dates can be dried in the sunshine. Peas can be dried in special ovens.

Dried milk and instant coffee powder are made by spray-drying. Liquid milk or liquid coffee sprays down through a tall tower. All the water evaporates from the liquid droplets as they fall, leaving behind the dried milk or coffee powder.

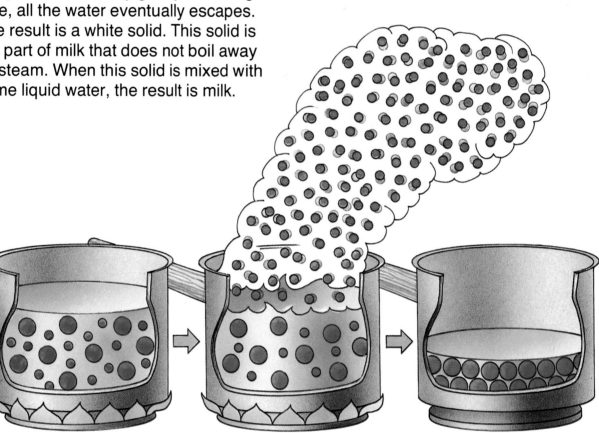

heat from flame gives energy to jam molecules

jam boils and water escapes as steam

level of jam goes down

Pasta with cheese sauce

Ingredients
4 oz pasta shapes
2 cups water
3 tablespoons dried milk powder
2 oz margarine or butter
2 oz plain flour
4 oz cheese
salt and pepper

Equipment
a large pot
a small pot
a tablespoon
a measuring cup
a wire whisk
food scale
a cheese grater
a plate
a colander

1 Ask an adult to help you boil a large pot of water. Measure the dried milk powder into the measuring cup.

2 Fill the measuring cup with water to the 2-cup mark. Stir until the milk powder and water are thoroughly mixed. Grate the cheese onto a plate.

3 When the pot of water is boiling, carefully add the pasta shapes. Boil without a lid for 10–12 minutes. Ask an adult to help you drain the cooked pasta through a colander.

4 Weigh or measure the margarine or butter and the flour very accurately. Put them into the small pot and pour in the milk. Mix with the wire whisk. The mixture will look rather lumpy at this stage.

5 Over a medium to high heat, whisk the mixture constantly as the margarine or butter melts, and the sauce heats up.

6 When the sauce has started to boil and to thicken, turn the heat down low and simmer for 1 minute. Keep whisking all the time.

7 Take the pot off the stove and add the cheese, salt, and pepper. Mix well until the cheese melts into the sauce. Add the cooked pasta, stir again and serve.

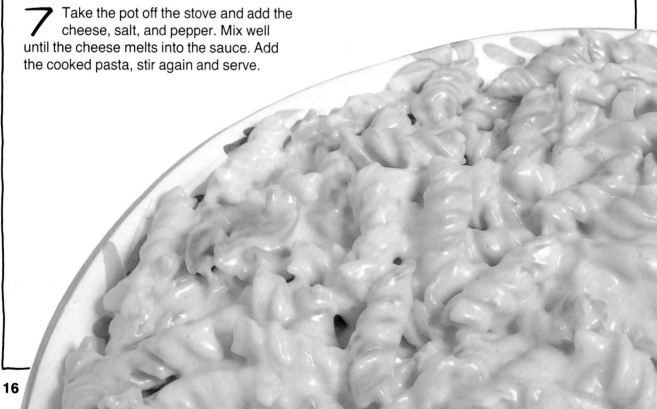

Measuring liquids

A recipe for bread will tell you to mix 25 ounces of flour with 10 ounces of water. The 25 ounces measure the weight of the flour. The 10 ounces measure the volume of the water. Volume tells you how much space is taken up by something.

You measure the volume of a liquid by pouring it into a clear glass or plastic container that has a scale marked on its side. A unit of volume is the gallon (3.8 liters). This can be divided into smaller units. There are 4 quarts (380 centiliters) in a gallon, and 2 pints (946 milliliters) in a quart.

- Dry quarts or liters are used for the volume of a solid.

- The volume of a cube of sugar is about 1 cubic inch (or 16 cubic centimeters).

Liquid measures

1 gallon	= 4 quarts (or 3.8 liters)
1 quart	= 2 pints (or .9 liters)
1 pint	= 16 ounces (or .4 liters)

Abbreviations

gallon	= gal
quart	= qt
pint	= pt
liter	= l

**1 quart
2 pints
32 ounces**

**¾ pint
12 ounces**

**½ pint
8 ounces**

**1 gallon
4 quarts
8 pints**

Making a solution

When you make a pot of tea, you pour boiling water onto the tea leaves and the water turns a clear golden brown color. This golden brown liquid is a solution of tea. The color changes because the water dissolves part of the tea leaves. This part is soluble. The leaves that are left at the bottom of the pot do not dissolve. That part is insoluble.

Salt is soluble in water. If you stir a spoonful of salt into a glass of water, the solid salt will slowly disappear as it dissolves. The result is a clear solution of salty water. But there is a limit to the amount of salt that a glass of water can dissolve. When the water cannot dissolve any more salt, it is saturated. Hot water can dissolve more salt more quickly than cold water.

Starch is insoluble in water. If you stir a spoonful of starch powder into a glass of water, the water will not dissolve the starch. The result will be a cloudy mixture called a suspension.

Many clear liquids that you can see through are solutions. Some solutions are made from solids dissolved in liquids. Liquid food colorings are solutions that contain powdered dyes dissolved in water.

Solutions can also be made from gases dissolved in liquids. Carbonated soda is a solution of carbon dioxide gas dissolved in sugary water. When you unscrew the top of a soda bottle, some of the dissolved gas escapes and the soda fizzes.

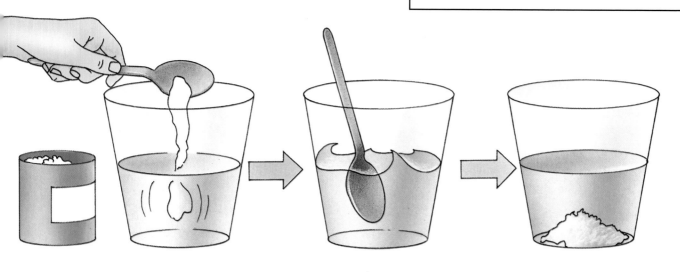

salt is added to water **salt dissolves in water to make clear solution** **no more salt will dissolve in saturated solution**

Butterscotch sauce

Ingredients
2 oz butter or margarine
4 tablespoons soft brown sugar
2 tablespoons Karo syrup

Equipment

food scale
a small saucepan
a tablespoon
a wooden spoon

I Weigh out the butter and put it into the saucepan. Measure the sugar and add it to the pan. Do the same with the Karo syrup.

2 Heat the ingredients gently. Stir them with a wooden spoon until the sugar has dissolved and the butter has melted.

3 Make sure that the ingredients are mixed together well. Bring the mixture to a boil and let it bubble for 1 minute. Serve at once with ice cream or pudding.

Filtering

You cook frozen peas by boiling them in water. The water is then removed by straining the peas in a strainer. The water drains through holes that are too small to allow the peas to pass. The peas stay behind in the strainer, which works as a type of filter.

A tea strainer is a filter. It has smaller holes than a strainer. As the tea pours through it, the tea strainer keeps tea leaves from passing into your cup.

A coffee filter made from paper is full of tiny holes that are too small for you to see. The filter holds coffee beans which

Ghee (Indian butter)

Ingredients
8oz butter

Equipment

a saucepan
a bowl
a piece of fine muslin
a strainer

1 Melt the butter in the saucepan over a medium heat. Do not let it bubble or burn.

2 Place the strainer over the bowl, and line it with the muslin.

have been ground into a gritty powder. When you pour boiling water onto the ground coffee, the water dissolves the taste and smell from the powder. The water then passes through the paper filter. Clear brown liquid coffee drips down into the coffee pot.

Some Japanese teapots are fitted with a filter in their spout. The filter is a bundle of thin twigs that trap the tea leaves as they enter the spout.

The water that comes into our homes has been filtered at a water plant. The filter is a huge tank that has a layer of stones and sand in the bottom. Water pours into the tank and passes down through this layer. The sand filters the water and traps any solid particles in it.

3 Carefully pour the hot butter through the strainer into the bowl. Discard the white pieces that remain in the muslin. When the ghee cools, use it to fry spices, meat, and other ingredients in Indian recipes.

What is density?

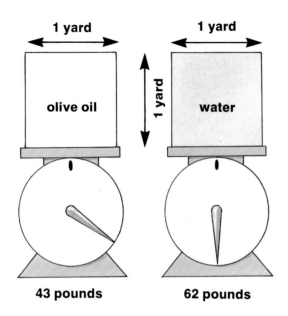

1 yard — olive oil — **1 yard**

1 yard

water

43 pounds　　**62 pounds**

Which is heavier – cooking oil or water? The answer depends on how much oil and water you measure. You must compare equal volumes of oil and water in order to answer the question.

Scientists compare different substances by measuring the mass of 1 cubic yard of each substance. They call this the density of the substance.

The density of water is 62 pounds per cubic foot. This can be written as 62 lb/ft^3, for short. Olive oil is less dense than water. Its density is about 43 lb/ft^3.

Layered lemon Jello

Ingredients
1 3oz package lemon Jello
1 cup boiling water
1 cup cold water
2 eggs

Equipment
a small bowl
a measuring cup
a tablespoon
an electric mixer
a large bowl
a glass serving bowl or dishes

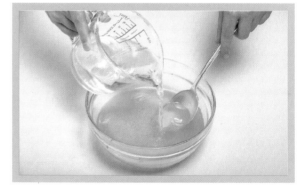

1 Ask an adult to boil 8 ounces of water. Pour the package of Jello into the bowl, and ask an adult to pour the boiling water into the bowl.

2 Stir until all the Jello has dissolved into the water. Add the cold water to the Jello and stir. Chill the bowl of Jello in the refrigerator for 30–45 minutes.

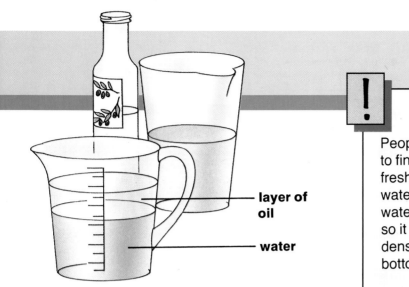

layer of
oil

water

Oil floats on water. Any substance that is less dense than water will float. Any substance that is more dense than water will sink.

3 Separate the eggs. Place the whites in the large bowl and beat until stiff. Take the Jello out of the refrigerator and add it to the bowl of egg whites.

4 Mix together with a tablespoon and pour the mixture into the serving bowl or dishes. Return the Jello to the refrigerator for at least 2 hours until set.

What is surface tension?

Have you noticed how water drips from a tap? Each drop does not break up as it falls, but it collects together into a round shape. The surface of water, or any other liquid, acts as if it has a skin. This is called surface tension. It is caused by the molecules in the liquid's surface pulling toward each other.

The surface of the water in a glass tumbler is not flat. The water curves upward where it meets the sides of the glass. The water molecules and the molecules in the glass pull toward each other. This attraction between the water and the glass makes the water pull itself upward.

A cloth is made from long thin fibers that are packed close together. Cloths soak up spilled liquids because surface tension pulls the liquid up into the gaps between the cloth's fibers.

molecules at surface of drop pull toward each other

!

Sprinkle a few drops of water onto a greased cookie sheet. Surface tension holds each drop in a tight round shape. Now lightly wet the end of a matchstick with dishwashing liquid. Gently touch a drop of water with the stick. The drop immediately loses its round shape and slumps downward, spreading over the cookie sheet.

Dishwashing liquid is a detergent and causes the surface tension of water to become less. This helps water to mix with grease and to clean dirty dishes.

Mixing liquids

When you make a French dressing for a salad, you shake together a type of salad oil, such as sunflower oil, and vinegar, and flavorings. This kind of mixture is called an emulsion. It contains droplets of oil which usually spread out through the watery vinegar.

Oil and water do not mix because the different molecules do not cling to each other. When you leave a jar of French dressing to stand, it slowly separates into two layers. The top layer is oil, which is less dense than watery vinegar.

Milk is an emulsion of fat droplets in water. The fat separates when the milk turns sour. Salad cream and mayonnaise are also emulsions.

You should not leave homemade mayonnaise for too long after making it. Mayonnaise contains an oily part and a watery part, which soon start to separate.

The mayonnaise that you buy in a store keeps for much longer. It contains added ingredients called emulsifiers or stabilizers. They help the molecules in the oily part to cling to the molecules in the watery part. Emulsifiers stop the droplets of oil from joining together and separating from the watery part.

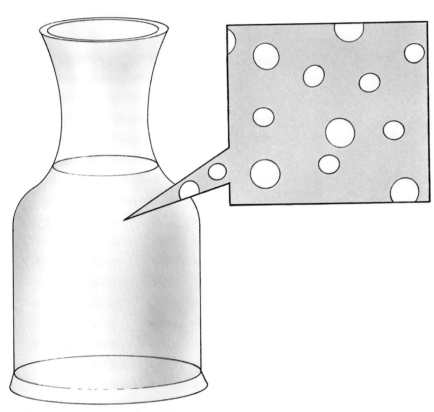

oil droplets spread out through vinegar in an emulsion

oil and vinegar droplets separate into two layers

Winter salad with dressing

Ingredients
8 oz white cabbage
8 oz red cabbage
3 celery stalks
mustard greens
½ teaspoon dry mustard powder
½ teaspoon salt
¼ teaspoon pepper
3½ fl oz sunflower oil
1 fl oz wine or cider vinegar

Equipment
a cutting board
a knife
a large bowl
a pair of scissors
a colander
a tablespoon
a teaspoon
a fork
a measuring cup

1 Ask an adult to help you slice the cabbage finely. Wash the sliced cabbage and put it into a large bowl.

2 Wash and chop the celery. Put the chopped celery into the bowl.

3 Use the scissors to cut off the mustard greens. Put them in a colander and rinse under cold water. Drain, and then add the mustard greens to the bowl.

4 Put the dry mustard, salt, and pepper into the measuring cup. Add the oil up to the 2½-oz mark.

5 Now add the vinegar up to the 3¼-oz mark. Whisk with the fork to blend together all the ingredients.

6 Pour the dressing over the salad. Mix well with the fork and spoon so that all the salad is coated with the dressing. Serve as soon as possible.

Acids and alkalis

Vinegar and lemon juice have a sharp taste. This is because they both contain substances called acids. Acids dissolve in water to make solutions that are acidic. Your stomach makes an acid that helps to break down and digest your food.

When you have too much acid in your stomach, this can cause indigestion. Some people eat antacids to relieve their indigestion. These tablets contain substances called alkalis. Alkalis dissolve in water to make solutions that are alkaline. The alkali from the tablets fights against the extra acid in the stomach and takes away its effect. The result is water and a substance like salt. Water is neither acidic nor alkaline. It is neutral.

You can use the colored water from boiled red cabbage or beets as an indicator. Pour some colored water into five glass jars. Stir one of the following into each jar: lemon juice, vinegar, bicarbonate of soda, baking powder, and soap. Make a note of the color of the liquid in each jar. Try to figure out which substances are acids and which are alkalis.

The acids and alkalis you use in cooking are weak, but others are dangerously strong. Car battery acid can eat through metal. The alkali in oven cleaner can burn skin.

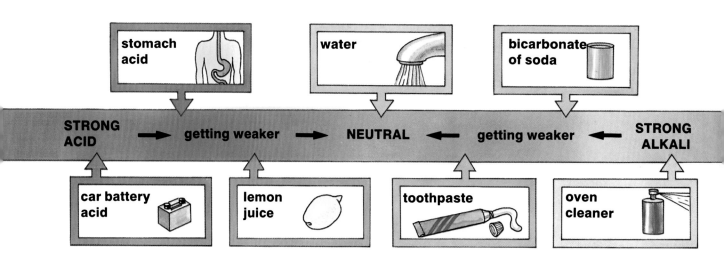

Scientists use special dyes, called indicators, to find out if a solution is acidic, alkaline, or neutral. An indicator changes to a different color, depending on the kind of solution it is placed in.

Carbonated lemonade

Ingredients

2 lemons
1 pint water
2 tablespoons sugar
½ teaspoon bicarbonate of soda

Equipment

a grater
a cutting board
a lemon squeezer
a measuring cup
a 12-oz pitcher (to serve)
a tablespoon
a teaspoon
a knife

1 Wash the lemons well. Grate the outer yellow rind on a fine grater. Put the rind into the glass pitcher.

2 Cut the lemons in half and squeeze out all the juice. Add this to the pitcher, making sure you leave the pits behind.

3 Measure the water and add it to the pitcher, together with the sugar. Stir until the sugar has dissolved. Taste the lemonade, and add more sugar if it is too sour.

4 Stir in the bicarbonate of soda and serve at once, while the lemonade is fizzing.

Further things to do

Take two identical plastic bottles and half fill each one with water. Dissolve a tablespoonful of salt in one bottle. Place both bottles in the freezer. Check as they begin to cool. The bottle of pure water will freeze first. The salty water freezes later, when the temperature has fallen. Solutions freeze at lower temperatures than pure water.

To show that vegetables contain water, seal some fresh lettuce leaves inside a plastic bag. Place the bag on a sunny windowsill. After a few hours, the inside of the bag will be coated with drops of water.

Take a measuring cup and some glass jars of different sizes. Guess the volume of each jar in ounces. Then fill one of the jars with water. Pour the water back into the measuring cup to see how accurately you had guessed. Repeat with the other jars.

Place a blunt darning needle on a small piece of paper towel. Lay them carefully on the surface of some water in a shallow baking dish. After a few minutes the paper will sink, leaving the needle floating on the surface skin of the water. Now touch the surface of the water with the end of a match that has been dipped in dishwashing liquid. This reduces the surface tension and makes the needle sink to the bottom of the dish.

Half fill two glass tumblers with water. Put three tablespoonsful of salt into one, and stir until the salt has dissolved. Place a fresh egg in the tumbler of pure water, and then into the one filled with the salt solution. The egg sinks in the fresh water and floats in the salt solution. Salty water is more dense than fresh water.

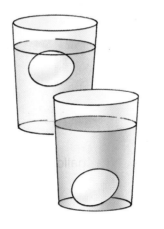

Glossary

acid
A substance that can make an alkali become neutral.

alkali
A substance that can make an acid become neutral.

atom
The smallest part of any substance. There are about 100 different types of atom.

boil
A change that happens when a very hot liquid bubbles and froths, and gives off a gas.

degree Fahrenheit
A unit that is used to measure temperature. It is written as °F for short. The scales of most thermometers are marked in degrees Fahrenheit.

density
A measurement that gives the mass, or weight, of 1 cubic yard of a substance.

dissolve
When a substance mixes into a liquid and makes a clear solution.

emulsion
A mixture that is made up from droplets of one liquid spread out in another liquid.

energy
Energy is a type of power that makes things happen. Adding heat energy to a substance makes it become warmer.

evaporate
The way in which a liquid slowly changes into a gas or vapor.

filter
A piece of equipment that is used to separate the solid pieces mixed in with a liquid.

indicator
A chemical that changes its color and shows if a liquid is an acid or an alkali.

insoluble
A substance that does not dissolve in a liquid.

mass
A measurement that shows how much matter is in something. Mass is measured in pounds.

matter
Everything in the world is made up from matter. Matter has mass and volume.

molecule
A tiny part that makes up most substances. Each molecule contains two or more atoms.

neutral
A liquid solution that is neither an acid nor an alkali.

saturated
When a solution has dissolved as much as possible of another substance.

scale
A row of marks with numbers that is used to measure something.

soluble
When a substance can dissolve in a liquid.

solution
A liquid that is the result of a substance dissolved in a liquid.

surface tension
An effect that makes a liquid behave as if it has a skin.

suspension
A mixture that contains a powdery solid shaken up with a liquid. The solid does not dissolve in the liquid.

volume
A measurement that shows how much space an object takes up. Volume is measured in gallons, quarts, etc.

Index